Ten Sticks of Dynamite

Dedicated to all the wonderful people I've coached over the years who have chosen to live differently, and from whom I've learnt so much

Ten Sticks of Dynamite

**To blow up your boredom
to blast your mediocrity
or just to boot you out of bed
tomorrow morning**

Andrew Sercombe

A LION BOOK

Published by
Lion Publishing plc
Sandy Lane West, Oxford, England
www.lion-publishing.co.uk
ISBN 0 7459 5028 0

First Edition 2000
10 9 8 7 6 5 4 3 2 1 0

A catalogue record for this book is available
from the British Library

Typeset in 12/18 News Gothic
Printed and bound in Great Britain by
Cox & Wyman Ltd, Reading

A Note from Me

You want to get up each day enthusiastic for life?

So do I.

You want to live life to the full, confident of who you are, where you're going and how to get there?

Me too!

I have chosen to enjoy being who I am. I want my life to be spontaneous, more creative, a bit more scary – and a whole lot more interesting. I want to live as free as possible from self-imposed inner limitations, and from the perceived or actual expectations of others.

I want to go beyond the ordinary, to be stretched by my own imagination, ambitions and ideas. I am thankful to say that I know where I'm heading in life, and God knows I need a lot of space and freedom to enjoy the journey! Stress for me is to be confined. I'm easily bored, easily intrigued – and not naturally calm. In fact the *thought* of being calm for too long is unattractive. I remember in my teenage years having a longing to be quiet and confident. I was neither, and although time and maturity have produced significant growth in both those qualities they are not my ultimate goals. What a relief!

Like most people heading somewhere, I have little expectation that I will 'settle' for long. I never was a settler – although I think I may have married one!

Andrew Sercombe
andrew@powerchange.com

Ten Sticks of Dynamite

Imagine getting up every day with the excitement of knowing that *anything* could happen!

Imagine getting dressed in your normal clothes *knowing* this is *not* going to be an average day.

Imagine wondering what today could look like as *you* decide to make it special, different, like no other day.

Ten Sticks of Dynamite is written for those who want to blow big holes in the boredom of ordinariness, who want to live with surprises and challenges that they cannot easily solve, pigeon-hole or rationalize. It is for those who want to see Change not as an enemy, but as a friend.

Dynamite is a powerful symbol of change. Only a century or so ago this chemical concoction changed for ever the known world, enabling people to build roads and rail links where they had never gone before, and to mine gold, blast stone and make weapons for defence and attack – in an unprecedented way.

Several of the 'sticks of dynamite' in this book have a slow-burning fuse: you won't see immediate explosive results, but be patient – those radical results will surely come!

I want this book to show you that you have available the power to change yourself and the world around you. If you don't avail yourself of that power and use it, then the world will conform you to its image, squeeze you into its mould, and you will become (or remain?) just another ordinary uninspiring and uninspired person.

Let me introduce you to those ten sticks of dynamite:

Dare	Hunger
Imagine	Accept
Believe	Connect
Play	Love
Drive	Enthuse

You were not designed to be a wimp. You were designed to be a competent, responsible and courageous person, who enjoys each day. You were designed to dare.

You have fears to face and longings to fulfil – some big ones, some small ones.

A big one

Explorers impress me. Ranulph Fiennes, for instance, who walked unaided across the Antarctic with a friend. Walked. One thousand miles. Minus twenty-three degrees centigrade.

He pulled all his food and other requirements on a sledge behind him. Fearless? No. Mad? No. Daring? Yes.

Ranulph's fury knew no bounds when he realized he'd forgotten the dogs.

A small one

Anna is a thoughtful and bright eleven-year-old. Her school technology project was challenging her. She was designing and making a small propeller-driven vehicle. She had designed it about twice the size of everyone else's. Several people around laughed at her: 'It's far too big!' Anna and I discussed the *real* challenge. We decided it was nothing to do with the design of the truck, but a battle inside her that she needed to win: to go with public opinion, or to stick with her original design. We discussed it as a class. She described the pressure she felt. Anna grew up as she chose to stay with her convictions – and several others discreetly enlarged their models too!

You can be daring. Fiennes stared out his fears. So did Anna. Both dared to battle with something that was 'obviously' ridiculous. They both won.

Dare to accept your potential

However old or young you are, you have loads of potential. You can read, you can think, you can communicate, you do a vast amount of different things. Accept your potential, and use it – because only YOU have it.

No one else can do what YOU can do.
No one else has the background YOU have.
No one else can make the contribution to life that YOU can make.
No one else has your friends, lives where you do or has the opportunities you have. No one.

It is up to you to take the courage you need to make each day different, to make this world a happier place, to laugh in the face of your fears.

So accept your potential. Accept that it is possible to change yourself and the world from where you are reading this book, right at this very moment. Accept it.

What have you done in the last few days that is exciting and demanding?
What have you done that has made a difference?
Wouldn't it be great to look back on the next twenty-four hours and see a different picture, perhaps one painted in brighter colours?
And it is TOTALLY POSSIBLE.

If I were to promise to give you £20,000 for every idea you came up with, how much would you make out of me? £100,000? £200,000? If it is possible to come up with ideas for

£20,000 a time, then it is possible to do it without the cash offer. The issue is not, 'I can't think of any,' it's a case of motivation! Come on, dare to accept your potential. When you do that you release a veritable explosion of personal power. Your confidence grows. You start doing things you've never done before. The 'magic' begins to work – and life becomes a whole heap more enjoyable!

Angela was on an assertiveness course I was running one Monday. At lunchtime we sat together and she described how trapped she felt in her lowly social services job. She was surprised when I refused to accept her view. She was not trapped by her *job* but by her *fears*, and when she faced them she would be free. I watched her face lighten and promptly fed her some more empowering truth. She was far more competent than she was ready to accept. We all know the temptation to accept self-made limitations, rather than to face the challenge of fulfilling our potential.

Dare to acknowledge your weaknesses

No guilt trip here, by the way. Don't get hung up on what you are weak at! Remember, weaknesses highlight strengths. They are more often than not our strengths *taken just too far*, or perhaps not quite far enough. See weaknesses in a positive light, and move on from them. Weaknesses often show up an area of your life that you would like greater satisfaction in. The most 'together' people know where they are weak and avoid leaning too hard on those parts of their lives until they are stronger. You can do the same.

You may need other people to help you where you are not so strong, so they can be what you are not. And you can bring *your* strengths to the places where *they* are weak. We all have strengths in different places.

Remember your potential and use it to benefit other people

What do you do about your weaknesses that hurts or damages others? Don't just hide them. Face your weaknesses honestly, and they will intimidate you less. Hidden weaknesses, and things you have done in the past and tucked away out of sight, often behave like a cancer. They seem insignificant at the time but, left untreated, they can grow and kill you. Plan a strategy to deal with them. Unsurprisingly it is often their hidden nature that presents the greatest risk. Decide to talk to a trusted friend (someone who will not spread gossip about your life) about the things you struggle with. It is surprising how releasing this can be.

Dare to fulfil your responsibilities

You have responsibilities to those around you: to those you are contracted to – an employer or clients, for example – to your children, your parents or both, and to society. Have the guts to face and fulfil those responsibilities. Don't duck out of them. See them as a major contribution to your own happiness and self-worth.

Dare to accept other people's humanity

Give those around you the space to be human today. You never know what they face, and they don't know what you have to handle. You may need to encourage them, or challenge them. You may need to warn them, or teach them. Do it with gentleness, courage, boldness and grace... all of which take guts!

Dare to swim against the current

Dead fish go with the flow. They float downstream at the mercy of the river.

Be prepared to swim *against* the current. Have the courage to determine your own destinations, and allow the current to sweep all the debris of life past you, out into the ocean.

Dare to swim *with* the current when you need to. Twice in one week I coached people (one nineteen years old, another twenty-nine) who had reacted against their parents. They wanted to prove they were able to think for themselves, and to get away from the conventions of their families.

This determination meant they would *always* swim against the tide, regardless of what they really wanted, because they were not going to do what everyone else seemed to be doing or expecting. Their lives were unhappy, and they still felt trapped.

Changing their minds, and forgiving their parents, changed their lives. Our minds are the easiest thing in the world to change once we realize that we can have something much better than what we've got.

Dare to accept isolation

Daring to be different will mean you will be a bit lonely at times. You will be misunderstood. You will experience a certain amount of rejection and conflict. Every significant agent of change has dared to stand out, to protest, to object, to reveal, to explore and to question. You will meet those who want to keep things as they are, and will oppose your ideas for the sake of their personal comfort and security.

Make sure that your desire to swim against the current isn't just an obtuse desire to be difficult, or to make someone else's life a misery. Check out your motives: is this for the benefit of *all*, or just for my *own* benefit? Is this going to *harm* me or anyone else?

Inner freedom

I sat at the feet of this old Chinese man in a discreet location in Beijing. He looked physically worn, but his spirit was vibrant and his face glowed.

'What', I asked him, 'was the worst thing about being imprisoned for twenty-one years for your religious beliefs?'

'The solitary confinement,' he said. 'And the lice.'

'How big was your cell?'

He pointed to the single bed in the hotel room. 'That big.'

This pastor had refused to deny his faith. He knew that inner freedom must never be sacrificed for outer freedom.

What about you? Will you just conform? Even when it means self-violation – going against what you know to be right?

What price do you pay to live free?

Imagine

Come with me to Wonderland. Wonderland is a place right near where you are. It is just the other side of a mystical door in your mind. (Little children go there many times a day!)

Come on then...

Welcome to Wonderland!

Here in Wonderland you can be bold or sensitive, confident or gracious, mad or sensible. You can be anything you like. It is a world of 'let's pretend' and allows you to walk out onto the stage of life however you want to be.

It's OK

It's OK in Wonderland. Wonderland is a world for little children and grown adults who want to enjoy creativity and amusement, and spark up lots of wonderful ideas. It is a world where no one is to blame, where it's nobody's 'fault'. We use Wonderland in developing the innovation and imagination of hard-headed business people who have mislaid their sense of fun and creativity at work. It's a laugh a minute – and yet deadly serious. Wonderland is a most productive place to visit.

On the next page is a Wonderland exercise for you to try:

You woke up this morning to find that you were the prime minister, or the president! After you had overcome the initial shock you decided you'd better get on with it. In Wonderland you can do absolutely anything, so which fifty things would you like to do at the wave of your magical Powerstick?

Lie back and imagine...

You can fly!

Imagine yourself no longer earthbound for a few moments. Imagine yourself to be a great bird, an eagle perhaps, taking off for a pleasure flight amidst vast peaks and snow-capped mountains. Upheld effortlessly by the awesome power of the fresh, crisp Wind of Opportunity, you soar, glide and climb to greater and greater heights, far above the valleys, some green, some cold and in shadow, some stretching beyond your vision; inhabited valleys with little specks of people living in wooden shacks, scratching a bare living from the earth.

It works!

We did the Wonderland exercise in a corporate training event that I led with a huge food manufacturing company – fifty managers and senior executives in a hotel conference room in the north of England. We came up with 600 answers to a current business problem they were facing. Six hundred! Some answers were totally impractical. However, some answers were very practical indeed. You can imagine how much fun we all had doing it!

You can dream up your own scenarios in Wonderland and play any time you like. Use it to solve problems at work, or at home to deal with challenges there.

You are above it all now, encompassed by and consumed with a passion to explore the vast potential of the Wind – learning to use its currents, learning that you need not use your own strength to drive yourself ever upwards, for by being tuned to the Wind and harnessing its power you can be lifted far above the limits of your own natural strength into a new dimension.

Soar on...

> 'Please do not ask "What is broken and how can we fix it?"
>
> 'Instead ask "What is possible and how can we achieve it?"'
>
> *Attributed to Kevin Gaskell*

Believe

Faith, the invisible substance of believing, has an amazing power. It is the confident assurance that something we want is going to happen. It is the certainty that what we hope for is waiting for us – even though we cannot see it up ahead.

Faith is like a jet engine that propels us into the future, enabling us to do those things we had no idea were possible for ordinary people.

Faith is spelt R.I.S.K. In fact faith and risk are twins – you can't have one without the other!

And like all the other 'sticks of dynamite' in this book, it costs something.

Risk your natural security

Like getting on a bus or train, you must leave where you are to get to where you want to be. You cannot enjoy hope for the future and still cling on to the present. Letting go is essential if you want to move on.

Letting go

A steel erector working high up on a huge skyscraper in New York lost his footing and started to fall. At that very instant he managed by some miracle to grab a swinging steel cable that was hanging loose, and he was left dangling precariously in mid-air by just one hand, hundreds of feet above the ground. Eventually, rescuers reached him and told him to let go of the cable so that he could be taken to safety.

Melvin decided on a dry run with the spanner...

He couldn't let go. His fear was so overpowering that he was physically unable to open his fist, yet his long-term safety depended no longer on holding on, but on letting go. Eventually a rescuer had to prise his fingers one by one from the steel cable and break his grip.

Try this:

Write down here something you have become afraid of:

....

Imagine the scene when you first remember feeling this fear. Convert the entire scene to a video that you can play in all sorts of different ways. **You are in charge of the video player**. Slow it down. Make it smaller. Turn the sound down. Edit the video. Add something you like better – remake the scenes the way you'd like them to be.

Run the remade video a couple of times, and switch it off. Look at the blank screen.

What has happened to the way you feel about it now? Is the fear more, less or gone?

Sometimes it is very difficult to let go, particularly of things that have begun to affect our sense of security.

During the English Civil War, a soldier was being chased through the night and came upon a well in which to hide. He climbed down the rope towards the water – and came to the end of the rope. Knowing that if he let go he would be trapped in the well and drown, he hung on for hours, until he could hang on no longer. He let go – and dropped six inches onto solid ground!

Faith is like that. You leap in faith, and find your fear has gone.

Risk your effort

Bed is a comfortable place to be! My mentor, Campbell, jokes that more people die in bed than anywhere else, so the less time you spend in it the better! Of course beds do have other distinct uses, but for the purposes of this illustration I will assume that bed is generally for people who are tired, ill or lazy. Only by getting out of bed will you enjoy a life of hope, joy and dignity. Faith in the future is worthless unless it is acted upon.

Arthur

Arthur won the lottery. He had keyed in the winning numbers and would have been able to enjoy the 4 million pounds if he had not, in a moment of – quite rational – unbelief, thrown away his ticket. It was good that he had the faith to buy the lottery ticket in the first place. (You need a massively huge quantity of faith to do the lottery!) But acting in unbelief robbed Arthur of his reward (it has a habit of doing that). He won the lottery, but got not a penny.

Risk your image...

... at least for now. For many people that is a big risk. What people think of them matters a great deal. Of course we would be a lot less concerned about what people thought of us if only we realized how little they did!

Why spend the rest of your life trying to conform to the real or imagined expectations of other people? Take the risk and walk beyond those expectations. They are designed to control you.

A personal story

I'm forty-nine and in my comparatively short lifetime have taken a number of leaps of faith – significant risks. Most of them were regarded with stunned disbelief by other people. I remember one particular decision which involved a major lifestyle change for us. I resigned from a very secure job as a design technology teacher to start and develop a church congregation in a country village. It cost me my salary, my security and my pension to follow what I knew deep within me was the right path for me. I was often misunderstood (and still am!) but the project was a success. It was worth it.

Someone who knew what we were doing at the time later came and apologized to me (after the success of the project!). He confessed that he had said to his wife, 'What on earth does Andrew think he is doing with his wife and children?' He didn't have the faith. He didn't believe it would happen. It wasn't him that *needed* the faith, of course.

Two sorts of people

We have learned over the years that there are two kinds of people: those who must see *before* they will believe, and those who believe first and *then* see. The interesting thing is that those people who take calculated risks, even though they may make mistakes sometimes, as I have done, or even get things thoroughly wrong, as I also have done, are the ones who achieve the most and change the world.

Tick the sort of person you would *like* to be:

Low risk: someone who sees and then believes.

Higher risk: someone who believes first and then sees.

Why I may find it hard to believe new things	What I could have instead of unbelief
I can't imagine them	A more developed imagination
The source may be unreliable	A reliable source
In my experience they are not true	Wider experience – there may be some truth in them
I have decided not to believe anybody	The freedom to believe some people
To accept them would be too painful for me	Adjusted rate of acceptance – a little at a time
I don't want to change	The huge advantages of changing for the better
I am afraid of my reactions – anger, tears, and so on	The dignity of self-control – and appropriately expressed emotion
I'm afraid of other people's reactions	Increased understanding of people and how to deal with fear
To accept them will hurt other relationships	Knowledge of how seeking truth can improve relationships
I want to stay 'innocent'	The wisdom and freedom of maturity

You can choose to take the things in the left-hand column and swap them for those in the right-hand column.

Risk trusting people

Faith is like a hot-air balloon: it has no visible means of support, but somehow manages to stay up regardless! Both hot-air balloons and faith work on some very real, down-to-earth principles, including trust, past evidence – and hot air! Even though we know that there are occasional train crashes, we have faith in the programmer of the destination board at the railway station – sufficient faith to trust our life to a rail company's drivers and staff; we get on the train. Faith by its very nature can have no guarantee and *must* have the potential for failing.

Risk letting go of what you have

Write down the three people you trust the most. Why do you trust them?

Sometimes it is hard to trust ourselves or others sufficiently to allow ourselves to change. Take a look at the table below to see why, and what you could have instead.

Travellin' Light

The hiker set off at dawn on his adventure to a distant destination...

... and returned ten minutes later to pick up one or two things he realized he hadn't packed.

He set off again...

... and returned a little later having recalled

something else that would be useful on his journey, but had been left behind.

He set off for a third time...

... and came back after some thought to recover those items that he sensed he would need after all.

By the time he had got all the essentials, his backpack was far too heavy to carry, so he decided it would be better to go 'at some other time'. He died defeated, but relatively comfortable. Do you want to live comfortably, but defeated?

What are you going to believe for?

Treat life as a game, not a war.

Life is sometimes a very serious game, a demanding game, a messy game, a painful game, a challenging game – but then so is rugby football. The difference between a game and a war is the relationship between the two sides. In a game they engage for the *pleasure* of everyone, including the 'opposition' and all the spectators and fans, within self-imposed rules. Winning is the plan, but losing is not life-threatening (usually!). In a war the intention is to

Albert had never had the ball before. He stopped to savour the moment, enjoy the experience.

forcefully impose our will on others, or to defend ourselves from such domination. The stakes are life and death; there are no boundaries, no limits. Wars are fought not for pleasure, but for deep personal freedom and rights.

Most of the time it is perfectly possible to turn life into a game. Even in the midst of war it is possible to have fun. Dream up ways to make life even more enjoyable – especially for others, not just you. Play the Wonderland game and see what you come up with!

Laugh at life

I *don't* mean treat life as a joke. I *do* mean milk it for its joy content. There is so much of life that has sparkle. Simply by looking at it 'through the eyes of a child' we see things differently. Life becomes intriguing in a different sort of way. We see it as simpler, funnier, with a sense of increased wonder – and some things are unquestionably hilarious.

Sit down with your friends and discuss what

you see as fun in life. The natural world is amazingly amusing. Can you think of anything more incongruous than a duck-billed platypus, or a gangly giraffe, or a kitten falling over on the floor, or a slug or caterpillar? Or little children exploring and learning about life? My wife Sue and I love watching lambs playing games out on the fields in the spring. How funny are they?!

What do *you* laugh at?

Laughter lines

Take a discreet look at the characterful faces of happy people. You may see 'laughter lines' – little creases in their skin from where their faces have expressed happiness, smiles and fun for many years. For some crazy reason some people want to remove these, trying to blend them out or tightening the skin so that they disappear. But laughter lines are a wonderful heritage. Perhaps they need celebration, not surgery.

Keep it simple

Life is better when it loses its sophistication. See the lighter side – without needing to ridicule others, demean, devalue or mock them. Live beyond constant vulgarity and innuendo. Upgrade the fun in your life by planning different things, and looking forward to them. Keep them simple. There is no need for huge financial outlay when it comes to fun. No need to be dependent on the TV either. You can double the pleasure by having fun creating your own amusement!

What will you do tomorrow that will be fun for everyone? Go on, make their day!

We want to hear from you!

We want your ideas for lightening the atmosphere at work or at home. Email us with your best suggestions, *duly tested out on your colleagues or family*, and we'll send you the whole collection when we've put them all together.

funagain@powerchange.com

P.S. You may even get your ideas in print in another of this series!

Does this mean standing over yourself with a whip like some slave master? Of course not! Drive is about *you* deciding that you are in control of your life and using that decision to good effect.

The drive to decide what lies ahead

Some things we cannot change. Most things we can. We can even change the weather. Of course, no one can make the sun shine, or stop it shining, but we can affect the climate precisely where we are. Put up an umbrella and stop the rain! Put on your coat and keep out the cold! Switch on the light and banish the night!

What lies ahead for you?
How can you improve it?
What 'climate' are you going to decide on?

The drive to begin

People who develop this drive to begin are the creators and innovators of this world. You can be one today if you are not one already. There is much less difference between imagined ideas and their reality than you think. The difference is beginning, and time. You want a university degree? You can have one. It may take you a

Buzz planned his shot carefully. He suspected that at 43.6 miles this might just be the drive of his life.

while, but for the vast majority of people it is quite possible.

I think it was in 1961 that President John F. Kennedy declared he wanted a man on the moon in the next decade. Asked how he was going to do that (the very thought was ridiculous to most!) he is reported to have said, 'I have no idea.' Yet in 1969 it happened. NASA astronauts even drove around the moon in a little 4x4 at one stage in the programme! It happened because a team and a nation were spurred on by a man of vision who inspired them to begin.

The drive to continue

Beginning is only the beginning. I have a friend who, from time to time, gets knocked down by life. As we discussed the buffeting of life he said, 'The trouble is, when I get knocked down I just want to lie there in the mud!' The longer you lie in the mud the more it seeps into your clothes and into your soul and destroys you. Lying in mud (emotionally or physically) eats away at your sense of personal value. We are designed to walk erect, with dignity, not lie in mud.

The drive to continue will get you out of bed in the morning and enable you to get past difficult obstacles. In her late teens my daughter

All or nothing?

At one stage in his farming career my dad took on a farm that he found out (too late) had very poor quality soil and produced virtually nothing. He woke up every morning anticipating a letter from the bank making him bankrupt and the family homeless. In the meantime he determined to continue with the farm and worked ninety hours a week to the point of emotional breakdown. He rescued himself and the family from financial ruin.

Just three years later the government assessors asked if they could use his farm as an example of what is possible: the soil in every field was shown to be in tip top condition and the farm a success story!

Elizabeth found that she had a very serious life-threatening disease. We were all devastated. Except Elizabeth. Through thick and thin, with many personal battles and tears, she determined to continue, refusing to let this wretched illness dictate her life. She is now one of the fittest people I know.

You can determine to continue.

The drive to finish

Many things can never be finished. We can never complete the task of curing every disease, or housing every homeless person, but the drive to finish will make sure we know where we are going with it!

By determining to finish the work you have begun, you will reap a great personal reward and an amazing sense of satisfaction.

Don't quit. Finish.

Hunger

Hunger will get you out of bed in the morning. It has a very motivating power. It did today for many millions around the world. Hunger drives people to go out and find food for themselves and their families. Hunger is a very powerful force – a sort of slow-burning dynamite.

Human beings have all sorts of hungers. Food,

'OK, the genie is out of the lamp and you've got one wish – **so what's it going to be?'**

The best time of the day for Adrian was always just before breakfast.

clothes, shelter, companionship and community are resources that we all need. Some needs are very basic, and we share them with animals and plants: nutrition and an environment in which we can thrive and reproduce. Other needs are much more sophisticated, and are to do with our deeper parts – spiritual, intellectual and emotional. They include needs for love, intellectual stimulation, order, creativity, physical contact and closeness, commitment, work, worship and a sense of personal value. For these we require an environment and a culture that promote the value of each individual to himself or herself and to society as a whole.

Hunger for freedom

We need space and freedom. Without them we are trapped.

Here is an old word for you by way of explanation: *yasha* – not a Russian ice-skater or ballet dancer, but the Hebrew word for 'save, rescue, help, deliver'. Its root meaning is to be brought into a wide open space, a place of freedom, a place where you can see all around you, so no enemies can creep up unnoticed.

Go for the wide open spaces of life. Dynamite has the tendency to make space for itself. Make sure you have the space you need to explore and live with freedom. If you haven't got it now, make it an ambition. Put a plan together for getting free.

Hunt for what you need

Hunting is about searching diligently. It is more than a casual look around, and involves careful pursuit of a missing or desired item.

For many animals hunting is literally a matter of life and death. As human beings we hunt too.

Hunting actually does get us out of bed in the morning. Where I live, people do not normally hunt wild animals or plants for their next meal, but they do hunt. They hunt for daily needs, for jobs or for the next contract for their business. Another modern-day equivalent might be the way people search through shops for food and clothes. Even today, hunting is still on the agenda and is essential for life!

Hunting for inner harmony

Built into every human being is a longing for inner satisfaction, and quite subconsciously we keep hunting for it. Our minds are searching for holistic harmony within our lives, for different parts of our lives to fit together properly. When they are out of balance, disjointed or clashing,

If you have never identified what you are looking for, do it now. Ask yourself: **'What do I hunt for most of all?'**

huge amounts of energy can be syphoned off behind the scenes of our thinking, and a sense of inner disturbance slowly becomes evident – disturbance that can result in poor concentration and upset sleeping patterns.

Hunting for wisdom

We need a great deal of information, and the wisdom to know what to do with it, if we are to live useful lives. But what sort of knowledge is useful these days? Do I need an array of certificates lining my walls? No! In fact yesterday someone suggested I *remove* a certificate from my wall. It did me no favours, he said!

Go for information *that will resource you personally*. All of us need to be as emotionally, spiritually, intellectually and physically healthy as possible. Search for assets that build up each area, for both yourself and others.

Emotional health

So you are able to laugh and cry without embarrassment (there's a time and place for both of these), confident in yourself as a person, knowing who you are and what you are worth, in control of yourself, strong deep down inside – not walked over by anyone.

Spiritual health

So you are able to respond to gut-level convictions and perceptions of life and the world.

God?

By definition, an object of worship is called a 'god'. As I write there is a revival of worship across the world, with many people finding that the highest possible god – God, the Designer of the Universe – can be known, loved, worshipped and enjoyed.

We are spiritual beings and we all worship something. Make sure the focus of your worship brings joy, forgiveness, inner satisfaction, release and a desire for the highest values in life. Healthy worship will release us deep inside, enhance our sense of eternity and deal with our fear of death. Choose the focus of your worship carefully. Aim high: you will become like it! You will want to be proud of the centre of your life. Avoid worship that leads to the devaluing of yourself or others, or brings uncertainty, fear of the future, or self-indulgence. Don't worship material things – not even people. They are too transient and not designed for such a purpose!

Intellectual health

So your mind is active, alert, free to explore, to decide, to think. Fill your mind with things that are true, noble, reputable, authentic, compelling, gracious. Focus on the best, not the worst, the beautiful, not the ugly, the things that are worth praising and will lift you up. Don't give space in your thinking to anything that may compromise your longing for 'platinum living' – a quality of being that enriches and builds on the most fundamental and important aspects of life. Reject thinking that is bitter, negative, damning or cynical. The first person such thinking cripples is you.

Physical health

So you are able to enjoy the exciting world around you to the fullest extent possible. Focus on being fit for what you want to achieve. There are so many opportunities to resource your physical life. There's no need to go to extremes, but do take advantage of them!

From the moment you were conceived you had a past and you had a future. As you look at your life you can see that the person you have become has been shaped and moulded, first of all by the decisions others made for you in the early part of your life, and then by the decisions you made for yourself. Both affect your future.

Not your choice?

Your existence was not something that you chose. Two other people decided that. (They did

Marcus faced his greatest challenge yet:
he mustn't turn out like his mother.

Take a clean piece of paper...

1. Make a private list of 'who you are' – the character and personality of the person you see in the mirror as you get up in the morning.

2. Put a tick by the things you like and want to strengthen.

3. Put a question mark by the things you wish weren't there, or you would like to sort out.

Write at the bottom of this list, this simple sentence:

'Today I accept who I am.'

SIGN IT.

not, however, choose your *entire* genetic makeup.) You did not choose your parents or your family; you were born into them. You did not choose your race, colour or original nationality. However, all these things, combined with your response to them and the merging experiences of the past, have made you who you are today. They provide you with a very important sense of identity.

For some people in our society, living with the results of their *own* choices is often easier than living with the choices *others* have made which affect them. Other people feel a sharp sense of pain as they consider the choices they themselves have made. They have no one to blame but themselves, and blame themselves they do.

Accept who you are now

Good or bad, right or wrong, better or worse, rich or poor, right now decide to accept yourself as you really are. Only that way can you do anything to improve your life in the future.

STAR credits

In my consultancy 'STAR' stands for Self-esTeem And Respect.

How do you know when you have done well? When people tell you. We can get too engrossed in our lives to notice when we are complimented. Shame. *Listen* to the compliments and give yourself some credit. Accept them!

When you feel that self-esteem deep down inside you rise a notch or two. You secretly feel proud of yourself.

Save up your 'STAR credits' and award yourself little prizes for what you have achieved. It works. Everyone around you will like you more as your self-esteem goes up; you will be less pressured and stressed, and each day will have greater joy in it.

Give loads of compliments to others, too. Don't do it to get something back. Pay a compliment simply because it's true. Compliments show that you have taken the time and developed the sensitivity to notice what the other person has done, and that you have the energy and courage to open your mouth and say so.

Self-esteem is a funny thing. When you behave in a way you admire in others, it increases. When you do things you secretly don't really like – or when others constantly do those things to you – your STAR rating goes down. People with high STAR ratings are popular and achieve a lot. All sorts of things are associated with low self-esteem; poverty, rejection, excessive weight gain or weight loss, addiction and depression are some of them.

Who are you at work?

Are you doing things at work that you feel are unworthy or unethical? Are you being asked to say and do things that you are uncomfortable about, or have to justify to yourself? Confront those situations. Find ways to stop doing them. Very little by very little they are damaging you, eating you alive.

Keep your STAR rating high; earn yourself those credits!

The final frontier?

One day you will not be around. You will not answer your phone, or dress in the morning, or go to work. You will have died.

Some people are so afraid of dying that they can't really live.

Millions of people are controlled by this fear. Although death is guaranteed to be one experience we will all go through, its ability to control us is phenomenal. In human beings the fear of death appears to be more than merely an instinctive longing to live, or a self-protective fear of the trauma of actually dying. For most of us, death is not an easy subject to deal with.

I was a minister of a church for a number of years and I dealt with death quite often. Death is far from all bad.

Here are some good things about death:

It is linked with new life. Every botanist will tell you that something has to die in order that its 'seeds' may live. Even in death, a tree or a plant can produce more fruit. When parts of me 'die' – arrogance, for instance – new learning can become a reality. When anger dies, reconciliation can be born.

Death is happening all the time – in fact it is far from depressing to realize that parts of our physical bodies are dying all the time so that they can be constantly renewed and updated. Death makes space for more life.

Death can unlock the future

The fear of death is hit on the head by a strong sense of destiny. Most of us have our own ideas

The Oak Tree

Imagine yourself as an oak tree for a moment.

It's Autumn, and the leaves of the oak tree – your old ideas, concepts and attitudes – having done their allotted task since springtime, need replacing. Slowly they lose their strength, curling up and turning yellow, then red, then brown. Their attachment to the oak tree is brittle and flimsy now. They have had an essential part to play but those leaves are not indispensable. Their essential death will provide fertilizer for future growth.

Soon the chill winds of winter will strip the old oak bare and it will stand gaunt and naked for a season. But it need not fear. It will not have lost its dignity. Soon Spring will come, new leaves will grow, and it will be stirred again to another year of fruitfulness and enduring beauty.

about death. Because of the strong Christian faith I have had for most of my life, I don't fear death. For me, death is not the final outcome; it is a gateway into a much better, perfect and eternal world, free from pain, rejection and unhappiness. I may not like the thought of the dying process, but I believe my ultimate destination is guaranteed and is actually arrived at by experiencing death. I don't want to sound macabre, but I'm looking forward to what lies beyond it!

Living is great. If you are prepared, dying can be too.

What is disappearing from your life?	**How may its death improve you?**
....	....
....	....
....	....

Connect

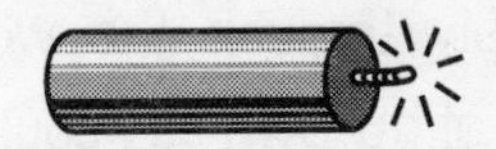

'He'll get a long way. He's well connected you know!'

'It's not what you know, it's who you know that matters.'

'The old boy network.'

Whatever we may think about preferential treatment or equality, the fact is we are more inclined to favour people whom we know (however well), and ones whom we have heard about through friends and acquaintances, rather than any anonymous person.

A personal story

I was forty-five before I started out in personal and corporate consultancy. By far the easiest way to get involved was to seek out the little connections that run invisibly through the world – and to create as many of my own as I could. It took ages to do it, years in fact. In some cases I am only just getting to work for companies that I contacted over three years ago. In that time the people who commission work from people like me (my potential clients) have got to know me by my unpressured phone calls and visits, and have learned that I am genuine, that I know what I'm talking about, and that I really do have something of value to them that they want. We have made a meaningful connection. They are wise to be cautious. I am wise to understand them.

Don't insult the crocodile

You will never live life to the full, or get to where you would like to be, without strong connections. You can easily start to build your very own network of personal friends and

Stanley let himself go for a moment. After all, nobody was watching...

'business friends'. Treasure them – treat them well. My business friends are, of course, real people with their own lives and families, and some of the business people I have grown to know have become my personal friends too.

Deliberately grow the little threads that join you to other people until those threads are strong. Be careful not to offend people unnecessarily. We all know it takes a lot to gain a friend and a lot less to lose one. As an old proverb says, 'Don't insult the crocodile until you have crossed the river.' I would suggest you don't insult the crocodile then either. I have learned by bitter experience that you never know when you will need to come back to his patch of the river at a later date. As they say, it's a small world, and that crocodile knows lots of other crocodiles on the river!

Listening

My job involves a lot of listening, but I'm not a natural listener. It hasn't come easily to learn those skills! However, good connections with others are made by listening to them very carefully indeed. It is so easy to be thinking of what to say next instead of listening properly to what the person is telling us. Listening is an act of giving. It is giving time and attention. It is tiring for someone like me to listen properly. I have to discipline myself to do it, although now less than I used to. I have become really interested in what my clients' lives and perspectives are. Those who come to me professionally want me to ask questions. That way they can be sure I am hearing what I need to know to help them. We say so much more than words can tell. Read between the lines when you listen next time, and look for little clues to what is behind the words. And don't jump to conclusions too quickly. Remember we see the world not as *it is*, but as *we are*. We interpret the world of others through our *own* understanding of it, and it is all too easy to jump to an inaccurate conclusion based on weak information.

Listen with all your senses

The best listeners listen in lots of ways. We communicate to one another with what we wear, the way we walk, the way we travel, our choices of furniture, the things we eat, the perfume we use. Learning to 'listen' to these signs is a skill well worth learning.

Fast Asleep?

Here is an exercise you can try!

We communicate even when we are asleep. Did you know there is much you can learn from a sleeping person? Try it.

What do each of these things tell you about them?

Where did they choose to sleep?

What are they wearing (or not, as the case may be!)

How are they breathing? Fast? Slow? Regularly? Restlessly?

What time is it? (They may be asleep at 3.00 p.m. What might that tell you?)

Don't be too dogmatic, though. They may be restless because they have flu, or are about to visit the bathroom, not because they are highly stressed!

If you can learn so much when they are asleep, think how much you might learn when they're awake.

Just wait...

How often have you asked someone a question and not managed to wait for an answer? Next time you are about to ask again, stop yourself and say to yourself, *'If I just wait, they will give me the answer.'* They nearly always do! Instead of telling what you think that person ought to do, or whatever, ask them what they want to happen, or what they think the best way forward may be. Here is a very useful simple rule that will help you understand people better:

Listen carefully, then
ASK ANOTHER QUESTION!

It is arguable that love may keep you in bed in the morning, not propel you out of it! Certainly the kind of deep love that develops over years between two committed people is stunningly satisfying and an amazingly powerful motivator.

Manipulated by 'love'

Love is a very difficult subject to write about in a book. As an author I know that all sorts of people read what I have written. Your own life

Maurice especially loved traffic wardens.
This one looked particularly needy.

may be quite different from mine. In my personal coaching practice I meet people with huge needs. For some of them the words, 'I love you,' have lost all significant meaning. For some, 'I love you,' means unwanted sex; for others it may mean being pressured into doing or being something that they don't feel happy about. They may be manipulative words to make them stay with a person who abuses them.

True love

True love will not demand that you 'do what I want', or assume that my unfaithfulness will be OK because you will forgive me. Love is about giving, not demanding. It is about me making personal sacrifices, not expecting them from you, or my parents, or my son, or my daughter. We have grown to associate love with rights, contracts and sex, but love is more about a lifelong, day-by-day commitment expressed in a million different ways.

It can work!

Sue and I got engaged when Sue was just seventeen and I was twenty, and married a year or so later. As I write we have been privileged to enjoy several decades of happiness together, and the pleasure of watching three very special children grow up through university years with an enthusiasm for life. We know a little bit about love now – although there is always so much more to learn! The children know what love is too. They've watched it happen and live in its warmth.

I also know that, for myriad reasons, there are so many people who, up to now, have not been able to enjoy the sort of friendship we have as a family. However, today you can sow seeds of love and friendship towards others that *will* grow and give you back more than you ever dreamed. If you are not used to it, start slowly and deliberately. Decide and begin. Find creative ways to make another person's day, to notice people, to treat them kindly. What I'm trying to say is love them – and watch what happens.

Try this exercise:

Disable yourself by locking the thumb and first finger of your writing hand together with tape or an elastic band. See how long you can stand the inconvenience. An hour? Two hours? A day?

Someone once described a community as a human body that works together. Think of three things this simple exercise says about the importance of people in your life and how they behave.

Enthuse

In Britain we can get a bit suspicious of those who appear enthusiastic – although we are secretly glad they are there to inspire us and take the rap when things go awry. Perhaps we admire those who are laid back, cautious, play it safe, or at least are calculating in what they do and think.

Enthusiasm isn't necessarily about being noisy or loud. Sometimes the quiet enthusiast is more influential than those who rant and rave. More steam to the wheels and less to the whistle, as the old steam-engine driver explained.

Harold was glad his ears had stopped him slipping further in and tried to remember what the salesman had said would happen next.

Enthusiasm is...

Refreshing

Enthusiastic people, simply because of their effervescent and sometimes unpredictable nature, often come up with great surprises. Some of these surprises are inevitably a bit scary. Most of them are wonderfully refreshing – and don't we just need refreshing ideas and creative sparkle!

Motivating

When did you last find yourself achieving something you would never have normally achieved simply because an enthusiastic person persuaded you to have a go at it? Enthusiasm is a key ingredient for leadership.

Empowering

Enthusiasm fires up parts of our brains that inject empowering chemicals into our bloodstream. It literally causes us to have more power in our muscles and more nourishing blood where it's needed!

Catching

An enthusiast is excited about life, and other people catch that excitement, putting their energy alongside his or hers. Do us all a favour by spreading enthusiasm liberally around you. It will cost you a bit of your own energy, but the gains far outweigh the losses. There is only one thing more infectious than enthusiasm – a lack of it!

Filling the gap

I don't have what it takes to live life the way I want to live it. I am not blown out of bed *every* morning determined to revolutionize the world! There is a shortfall between who I am and who I want to be.

I am filling that gap with God. I need him!

I believe that God is the designer and sustainer of the universe and of our world. I believe he continues to be interested both in its development and in you and me as part of it all.

I believe that it is possible for each human being to enjoy a vibrant, empowering, spiritual connection to God. I believe that the connection is readily available to all who dare to seek it, and that without it we are depleted.

I have made the connection. God is the calm in my life, the inner security I know I need. He is my inspiration to live differently.

Andrew Sercombe is a Powerchange$_{TM}$ Master Practitioner and Trainer. His consultancy, Rock PCD, serves a broad spectrum of individuals and businesses in the UK, inspiring personal success through expansive professional coaching and 'Gain without Pain' dynamic improvement strategies. 'I coach people who want to discover themselves, their potential, and what life has to offer.'

Andrew is married and has three children in their twenties.